Benny the Adverb

Written by Coert Voorhees
Illustrations by Powerhouse Animation

Meet the Parts of Speech

I name a specific person, place, thing, or idea. It's a big responsibility, naming things—a responsibility that requires a certain attention to detail.

Vinny the Action Verb

Some people say I'm all over the place. Some people call me a ball of energy. I take that as a compliment, because I just like to go, go, go!

I take the place of one or more Nouns or Pronouns. I always want the Noun's job, and I hang out with the Verb and Adjective.

Lucy the Linking Verb

I'm perfectly happy to link Nouns and Pronouns with the appropriate Adjectives, but it's not like I'm going to expend a lot of energy doing so.

I modify a Noun or Pronoun. I tell what kind, which one, how many, or how much. I pride myself on being the most artistic of the parts of speech.

Connie the Conjunction

Gather 'round everybody and let's have ourselves a wonderful time. I just love bringing words and groups of words together, don't you?

I modify a Verb, Adjective, or other Adverb. I tell how, when, where, to what extent, and under what condition. I often end in –ly, but I don't have to.

Izzy the Interjection

I express emotion!! Yep, I'm always here, always ready with my commas and exclamation points, just in case.

They call me Preposition because I'm pre-positioned. I'm first. At the front. Before every other word in the phrase? Got it?

I am a chameleon. A spy. An undercover operative. I infiltrate the sentence and act as whatever part of speech suits me.

BENNY THE ADVERB

Graphic Design by Mckee Frazior
Printed by Friesens, Altona, Manitoba, Canada

This book is typeset in Komika Text

Distributed throughout the world by Ingram Publisher Services
www.ingrambook.com

Printed in Canada

Benny the adverb loved to modify verbs, adjectives, and other adverbs.

He told the verbs where to go.
Vinny, return those books over there. Then come back here.
Grammaropolis Library
sci-fi
mystery
fiction

He reminded them when to do important things.
Brush your teeth daily.

Benny sometimes modified the adjectives he came across.
Is my soup salty?
Too salty. Obnoxiously salty! Make it less salty.

Occasionally, he even disagreed with other adverbs.
This platypus is very cute.
I think it's hardly very cute at all.

Honestly, he was pretty bossy.
I'd like my food now.
Uncool, dude.
But he knew the citizens of Grammaropolis needed him.

Vinny tended to drive enthusiastically.
You must drive cautiously.

Jake was often afraid at the movies.

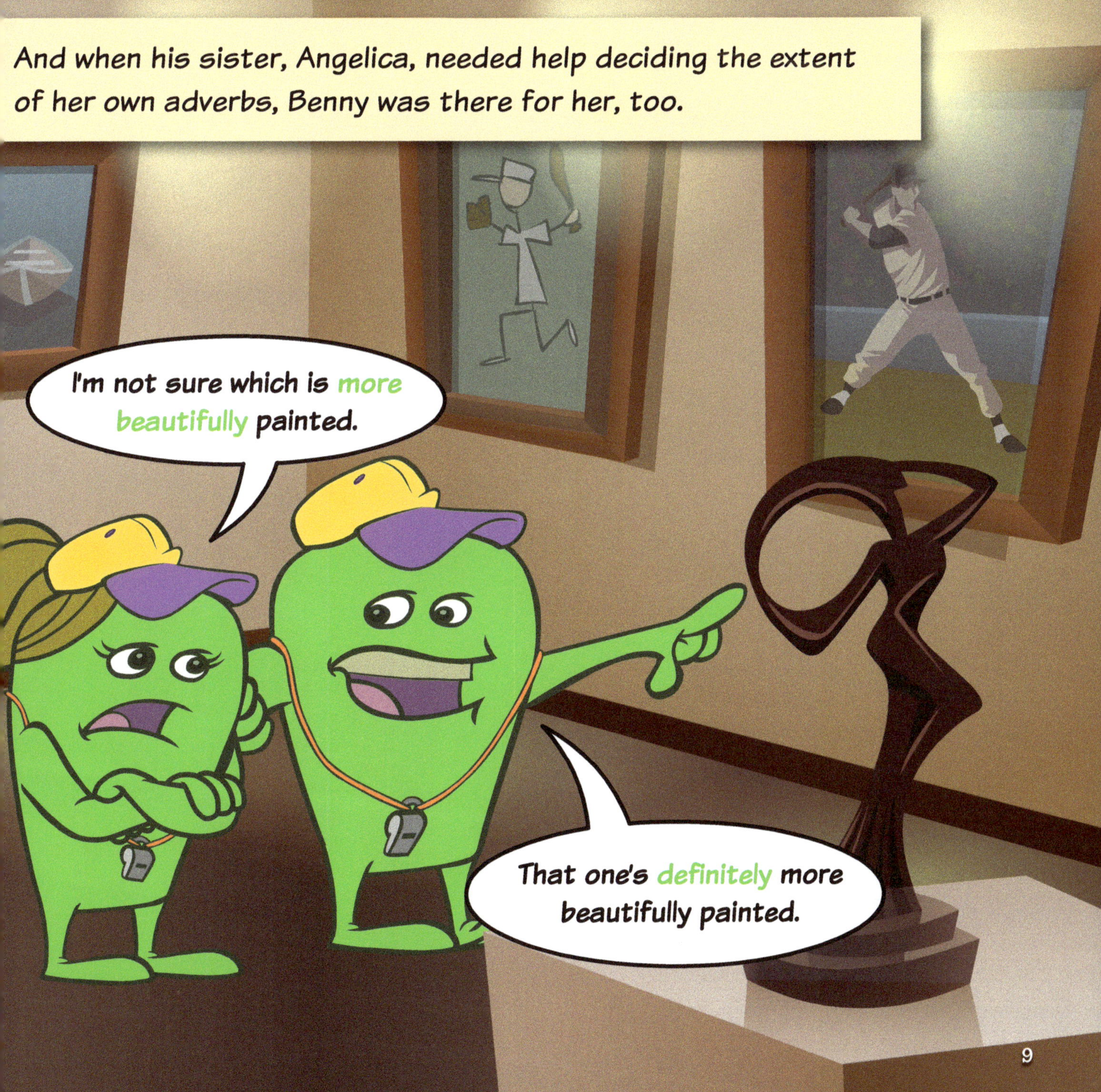
And when his sister, Angelica, needed help deciding the extent of her own adverbs, Benny was there for her, too.
I'm not sure which is more beautifully painted.
That one's definitely more beautifully painted.

Yes, Grammaropolis was in good hands with Benny.

Drive safely.

Be very careful.

Live happily!

Smile the most broadly!

And life was good. Quite good, in fact.

Until one day, when disaster struck.
This box is terribly, unexpectedly, and alarmingly empty!

His highly prized rock collection had been stolen.
Don't ask me. I'm just taking the guard's place.
SECURITY
Where is it?

SECURITY
I thought this was supposed to be a maximum security facility.
Nope. Just security.

Benny had no choice but to begin an investigation.
Where should we start?
We must look here, there, and everywhere!

First, Benny established a timeline.
When did you last see my rock collection?
It was here yesterday.
SECURITY

Then, with the help of Li'l Pete the preposition, Benny searched under the table.
Let's look inside the boxes, too.
My lock is here!

Connie the conjunction came over to help.
I'm investigating so intensely.
And?
I will continue relentlessly.

Then Angelica chipped in with a comparative adverb of her own.

Let's look harder.

Fortunately, that's when Benny found a clue.

It's a note!

Benny had been so focused on giving adverbs to others, he'd forgotten to save some for himself.

This called for a superlative adverb.
You are my most helpful friends.
Totally, bro. Totally.

So Benny offered to treat them all to some freshly squeezed lemonade.
Everyone buckle up safely. And Vinny, remember to drive...
Slowly!

Modifications: Verbs, Adjectives, & Adverbs

ADVERBS

An adverb modifies a verb, adjective, or other adverb.

I usually end in -ly, but I don't have to.

MODIFYING A VERB

Speak softly and carry a big stick.

MODIFYING AN ADJECTIVE

My classmates are incredibly silly.

MODIFYING ANOTHER ADVERB

Hector left the haunted house screaming quite loudly.

HOW

An adverb tells how.

The fire spread quickly.

I landed awkwardly when I fell off the trampoline.

EXAMPLES

quickly
awkwardly

WHEN

An adverb tells when.

EXAMPLES

tomorrow

always

WHERE

An adverb tells where.

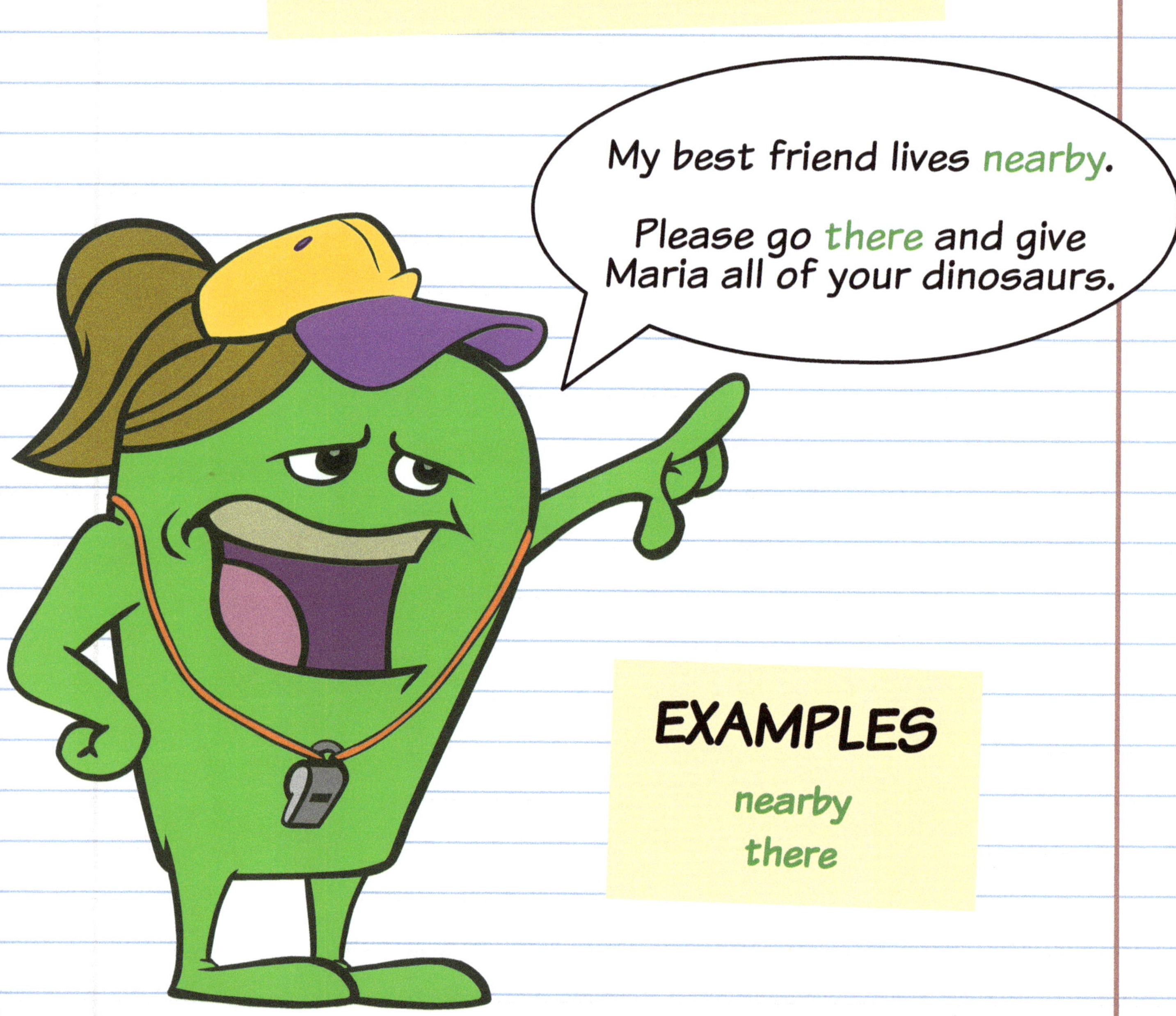

EXAMPLES

nearby
there

TO WHAT EXTENT

An adverb tells to what extent.

I hardly touched my chickpea mousse!

EXAMPLES

completely

hardly

ADVERB CLAUSE

An adverb clause is used to indicate under what condition something will take place.

EXAMPLES

if we try hard

Unless she studies

COMPARATIVE ADVERBS

A comparative adverb is used when making a comparison between people, places, or things.

EXAMPLES

faster
less

SUPERLATIVE ADVERBS

A superlative adverb indicates the extreme quality of something. It is used when talking about three or more people, places, or things.

EXAMPLES

most
least

CPSIA information can be obtained
at www.ICGtesting.com
Printed in the USA
BVHW051324130519
547997BV00001BA/2

9 781644 420102